WORKING THE ROOTS

Working the Roots

Amanda Bennett

QUERENCIA

Querencia Press – Chicago, IL

QUERENCIA PRESS

© Copyright 2025
Amanda Bennett

ISBN 978 1 963943 43 6

www.querenciapress.com

First Published in 2025

**Querencia Press, LLC
Chicago IL**

Printed & Bound in the United States of America

CONTENTS

Like Blood for Flowers

My uterus clenched tight
as a baby's fist calls me
with its silent cries at dawn.

Alone I pull the cup of peaceful blood
from the soft pinkness of my vagina
and see food.

A friend told me that our menses produce the only nonviolent
blood because it leaves our bodies willingly.

The blood of our cycles is worth more than money
because it contains vital minerals:
magnesium, potassium, sodium.

I hold my liquid self in my hands and
marvel at the nourishment I've made.

I am so thick
so rich
so dark
so red.

There is so much of me
I am hard to dilute.

I pour half a gallon of water
into my separate self and feed the plants
I call my children.

This is how it feels to be fed as you feed
to finally know the satisfaction of hunger

I offer the taste of lifetimes
my blood only knows.

Blood is a Reflecting Pool

I see myself on the outside
for the first time in three months
in the contents of a silicone cup
I wedged in my vagina overnight.

I released myself in sleep
softly knowing how long I've waited
for this red slide of letting go.

I see all the clouded dreams I've had
in the crimson murk of my body's goodbye

goodbye you
goodbye time
goodbye rue
goodbye child

who never lived like the rest of us yet.

Every few months I get gone a self
incomplete and too shy for life.

I pray this piece of me the kindest farewell.

How hard she worked to feed the possible
and find the fullness I once forgot.

god is in the nectar

i went looking for the god within and felt the sweet slide of nectar between my
lips   who is this liquid i am when i feel pleasure   connection   intimacy
vulnerability   who am i when i am close to her   when she touches me   when i
forsake the wall of safety for the valley of the unknown   i pull back my fingers
and make a v to stretch my liquid self   i know i only go this far when an egg is
close to coming   i can go farther when i am close to life   i put my fingers to the
sun to catch myself in the light   right now i am iridescent   all the colors at once
when i am like this i am a prism waiting to refract the light of other suns   that is
why i am here   to crack wide the sun of another through the push of my lips
ntozake shange once said she found god within herself and loved her fiercely
so i know i must find her too   guided by the love of my own waters   love is a lot
like water   flowing   renewing   a reflection of ourselves   when i touch myself
under the hood   directly on my clit i feel god in this tiny impermanent peak
blood will build us a mountain that dissolves when it is no longer needed

there is no permanent path to god   feeling is the only way

holograms in the buttermilk

my girlfriend and i are the only two flies at this buttermilk gathering and again
i feel the change   i am brighter   peppier   wittier   it's all a part
of keeping things light   i didn't dare notice the difference before loving her
what was the point of otherwise when i was the only one   i was used to
laughing from my chest   smiling with no eyes   and posing as if
the room was a camera   i thought being unreal would keep me safe
nobody hurts a hologram   but then i found her and learned how good
blackness feels when it's intimate   when it multiplies   i want to laugh from my belly
because it is the source of all life   being black in quiet places with her
brought me back from the nowhere i was   what must change
to make room for living

knowing is a moment

it's pride in raleigh so i take some shrooms before meeting lou and lie
on my couch in a frenzied stupor clutching my belly my oldest foe i
feel the rush of splendid bile that is the experience of coming up and
forget that fat is a word with meaning so i am all that's left in its place
words don't mean the same when you touch yourself i felt the soft skin
so hard this time i knew my daughter with closed eyes   the only way
anyone ever really knows anybody   she isn't a person yet because she is
only colors   i want to learn her pigment   it was a revelation to me
that this tangle of yellow light only became mine when i accepted myself
for a moment   what we love comes most freely to a self cracked open
with joy   in accepting what is i prepare myself to receive the mystery of what
could be there is nothing more mysterious than what i am inside i love most
the egg which will not let me go   in this life i will make myself a home
for all who wish to stay

we came from wholeness

i'm still on shrooms when lou opens the door and welcomes me into her first
free home   she's wearing a white button-down and black tie and walks me toward
her carefully curated rainbow of finger foods   in her kitchen we recall the years of
quieting our queerness through control
if the buttons and cuffs and colors are all just right
there is nothing out of the ordinary happening inside our impossible suits
at the table lou remembers giving birth and meeting her sons for the first time
they came into the world whole and perfect she said   and then i understand
how a child could be a second chance   i want to remember being whole
babies have no memory of buttons or cuffs or organized colors
anything they imagine is what is   our only task is to listen

black is a place we carry

black is a place we carry like the tiny polaroid lou took of us that i keep
in my wallet   sometimes i take it out and look to remind myself of a day
i felt close to everybody because i was safe with you   the picture took
so long to develop   for a while we were just faint strokes of memory
in a frame of white milk   we were there i knew underneath it all
but the pregnant gap between the moment and the memory it becomes is
a particular canal of agony   i know i'm black in all my memories
but who was i in the moment   i am so fond of that picture
of us because it is weightless   soothing   familiar   how much
of my face will i choose to carry in this life   just enough to know i'm home

The First Night

We leave at nightfall
when pleasure is our sole name
carrying only our market greens
and eggs uncooked in our bellies.

Your smile is brightest in the dark
when it is just us two half-sleeping
half-saying the spell of the rest of our lives.

Our packs are small because
we must be light. There is no room
for the hurt so old it yellowed
or the worry so worn it frayed.

What we carry is only as old as
our youngest dreams long-lost but
remembered at our first kiss.

I forget nothing, everything with you
in your eyes' reflection I see
our first free sunrise.

The First Red Moon

By the light of the morning star you see
blood on our sheets and tell me
tonight will be a feast.

I make a meal from plants we fed ourselves
and invite all priestesses around.
Last night they saw the moon ready
for birth—her waters broke in our bed.

By nightfall they come up the hill
in rough-worn colors bearing
cakes baked in ash shaped like the
woman whose womb is the moon.

My little dove so bright sits center
of us all. In the bath of her miraculous
blood she becomes the evening deity.

I worship her as well as the rest
when I see with their eyes the woman
only I often know.

This first red moon in the wild holds my lover
up in ways I could not alone.

Loving is no lonesome act.
Every month I give her to the world
at dusk to replenish her light.

Difficult Women are Like Dynamite

Difficult women are like this: a little girl with eyes
        pinned to the floor head-down
                waiting for Mother to finish
                        the dynamite stick in her mouth.

                        Difficult women are just that: gnawed-on red bones
                            dwindling fast in the light.
        If you turn her upside down she will not weep
        nor sweat in yellow pools
                to flood that box called home.

Difficult women are just that: crystals
  aged hard and white outside
        inside the stick and bones raged red and cold
           from the first woman she knew
     whose tongue was its own light.

Difficult women know just that: old dynamite is dangerous
        enough to make her say
             no   to touch
                no   to friction
  no   to heat
        no
      to shock
because she fears the fuse.

Difficult women are like dynamite
             and like light
    and she likes when you light
        the fuse the blasting cap
            the braid that remembers
                the familiar eyes bound down enough
                    to withstand every demolition day
                        known by her mouth.

Black People in Space

Jupiter's rings only bring bad news:
something about a cheap brother drowning
in flood pants living in a floodplain washed away
in the coffin that cradled him from birth
strung with rotting streetlamps for stars
teasing venomous rattles for children who
tongue walls for the earth's forgiveness
pilfering existence in the meantime
from apricot paint chips that bear no juice
only blood in lonesome corners
forked like utensils in two-prong outlets,
dying.

What is it like to live life as a memory
a dark reminder ringed iridescent
by radioactive green
refused refuse gnawing on the sun-
bleached femurs of broken FEMA
promises looking for the bruise of dusk?

A woman in a skirt with a metal core is
all yours, if only you unzip—
which you won't, because you fear skin
just as you fear the shore
the lie of a reprieve from the current
when the land that awaits is no friend
just the reaper for crops
promised before the fall.

This Heat is for Feeling

The day is violet by the time we get back to our nest in the trees in new hampshire after spending part of the day on an illegal dock at a lake so beautiful I wished nobody owned it. But on the lake there are boats and people floating and waiting for joy to arrive in the hot gaze of the sun. We're waiting too but don't want to admit it because we're supposed to be happy with what we have and in that moment I realize in my body that I have anxiety. It shouldn't be a revelation to anyone least of all me but I think until that exact second in space I couldn't let it into my conscious mind because that would mean recognizing all the ways in which my life is just one tight tunnel of anxiety, one big fear of falling into the hole I've made for myself that fits just my body and not one ounce more. I sit next to you and we dangle our feet in the water and I try to stay in my body for five minutes, that's all I can take but we do it together for the first time and it's kind of nice maybe we should do this more often, yeah?

twenties child

i let the wand in deep enough
to bring light to dark places
where the mystery of me is invisible no longer
rendered real as my skin
on the ultrasound screen

i'm bleeding on the inside while
the white woman doctor takes the sum of me
this month i'm 34

i am made of children
who die away as quickly as years
in the black basin of my belly

everything here looks good the doctor says
healthy—fertile—*except*—she moves in me
to the side and a tiny moon appears in the
night sky of my womb

there—a fibroid tumor the size of my fingertip
lodged in the muscles of my uterus

this is the child of my twenties
a small hard clump of cells
that multiplied as i divided myself
that grew as i shrank from who i was

for this tumor i paid the price of forgetting
there is no knowing too costly to remember

Denial

When I am too afraid to begin
I shrink to the size of
my worst memory

The words I give are padding
surrounding a body I believe
is too tender and too fragile
to be known

Please don't see me
this tiny pile of women
I cannot forget
bound by the crush of
my only safety, the overcoat

But I am overheating
the warmth is suffocating
softness creeps beneath
my skin like a bruise

Everything is fine
until it isn't

To speak the hurt
will make it real

And I am no conjure
woman
yet.

Anger

It's here—the feeling.
A bloody show of white fangs
white knuckles and white-hot
hate

I worry I'll go blind
so I look at it halfway
seeing nothing.

I turn my head slowly
recalling my full range of motion

The world I made inside
my mind is not white but
the absence of color
and texture
and pattern

The true violation is this nothingness
that masquerades as white space

This feeling, this nothingness has taught me
lies: that the world has no shape
and never will.

But in anger is always truth:
the world takes the shape of my hands
and their wonder

So I build my loom and begin.

Bargaining

The price of the loom
is my mother's womb.

I can afford one
or the other
but never both

I spend my night hours with ghosts
those unruly misers
whose hardest bargain is life itself

I have what they do not
their
envy holds the shape
of my dreams

I wake in wet tatters mumbling
the ghost's only word:

If.

Depression

I go back to the white world
of light without letter or meaning

I say this time will be my last
but I am a woman in love
with the end

I know the story of this world
like a god in a Greek tragedy
where I am both absent from
and responsible for my downfall

I suck my Achilles' heel like a fetish
like bittersweet candy as I watch
the familiar film of myself

in the dark theater of my mind
"Don't go in there, girl!"
I scream at the white screen

quietly knowing I wrote her
the same act
each time

Acceptance

When the film is done I leave
to my loom that frame of loose
ends I touch and see

After the empty light
of the white screen and
the tang of my troubled heel
I am ready to handle the real

The melodrama of my memory
cannot compare to the worldly
weight of thread in my palms

I recreate the story of my body
inside the loom's forgiving frame

keeping green far from yellow and
entwining bright pink with indigo

When I weave I say
what goes and what does not
again and again and again
until I realize

I'm learning the shape of the world
through the work of my hands

The true meaning of control is flow

The feeling I feared is the same as
the universe: infinite, divine, and interconnected.

Mojo Bag

For so long I feared
this weight around my neck

Ruby-red like blood
softer than my own skin

I did not know from where
it came or why

I only felt it was both
part of me and not

In my 26th year the ancestors
became my familiar

telling me the weight was
a bag I could open

We enter each other
remembering a future world

There is a sea of women
holding up the dead

piles of papers soaked
in blood from the heart

an old quilt telling picture-stories
of Africa and mojo and
griots gone to rest

I see love in the shape of weary
hands and weeping bones

this world is an altar begging me
to worship not the weight
but the gift it carries

the mojo bag is my inheritance

I receive it all
wearing the power of
this prayer in a bag

what was unfamiliar can be no burden
when we allow all parts to be known

I am so weightless I could fly

I Was There in the Future

In the sound bath the first bowl rings and I drift into something that is like my face but in pieces. I start by identifying my body parts as separate—womb nose legs teeth jaw—but then those parts morph into images of me at every age I've known and I greet them when they wake from a cloud of white light. Hello hello I say to myself when I was two and had two pigtails and two parents and such a hunger for my mother's one breast. She smiles so much and is so giddy but there is a seriousness in her eyes as she tells me she takes in everything and that I'll have to remember that going forward. I embrace her and she leaves and then I'm facing my eleven-year-old self and to be honest I'm terrified of her because she's fat with tiny gapped teeth and broken off relaxed hair and she's everything I would spend the next two decades trying not to be anymore. In seeing her I admit she still lives inside and she's sullen so sullen won't talk to me at first when I ask what's wrong and then she says don't you see everything happening around you. She goes away and I see myself at thirteen and bulimically thin and she has learned the art of keeping secrets. She is so cocky so self-assured because she knows now how to throw up in silent places and kiss girls only in quiet dressing rooms if nobody knows it never really happened right? *Oh my girls* I cry and take them into my arms which are big enough to hold every me I've ever loved and I give my smallest self my breast the way I wanted from my mother. Holding them shows me my face at sixty. I have gray dreadlocks and a patterned coat and gosh she's beautiful and so full of light and at peace with herself as life blooms on in the background. She says she's my best friend and I start weeping on the table because now I know she needs me just as much as I need her and the only way we're going to get through this is together. She drapes me in a yellow coat made of light that lets me know she's always been there, will always be there. Yellow is the color of the solar plexus chakra and mine was depleted because some bad stuff happened to me in the past but at least I have myself to say that it's all going to be all right in the end.

rest is the part in the waterfall

through the part in the waterfall i saw my own face   for the first time
reflected back to me in the space between the water and the world i wished for
after quitting my life three weeks ago   and coming inside the warm wetness of
the jungle in these blue mountains   the tangle of memories that share my name
are coming undone in my hands   like shoelaces   like braids   like a fish's
rainbow skin   when i hold these scales in my hands i know that i was always
worth the weight   i stayed away from this place so long because i was afraid of
being alone   but to my surprise everybody came too   everybody i am followed
in the space of my footprints   in this land of rest i learned that we leave
footprints for those who share our faces on the inside   i want to learn my inside
faces   they come out against the rush of water like i did the first time i was
born   i am my mother's inside face   i know that now   i know that now   i
know that now   away from everybody except my inside faces i baptize myself
again and again and again and again in these cool quick waters until a portal
opens up like a cervix effacing and i step through with my big grown body like a
baby and wail as loud as my first cry   there is no shame in being born   who
says it only has to happen once   i'll be born as many times as i need to   not to
get it right   but to feel the force of remembering lives that were not mine   but
flow through me as easily as i once coursed through my mother's veins   when i
am at rest i am a nursemaid for the dead   giving self-sweet milk to spirits with
fast-drying throats   my breasts contain as much food as i let them   i give to
you only as much as I give to myself   where there is hunger there is distance
where there is scarcity there is fear   i will not fear this closeness of love   taste
my breasts and know abundance   milk was my first waterfall   my first mirror
my first feeling of love   my mother rested enough to give me life   i will rest
enough to give you life   and you   and you   and you   and you   and me